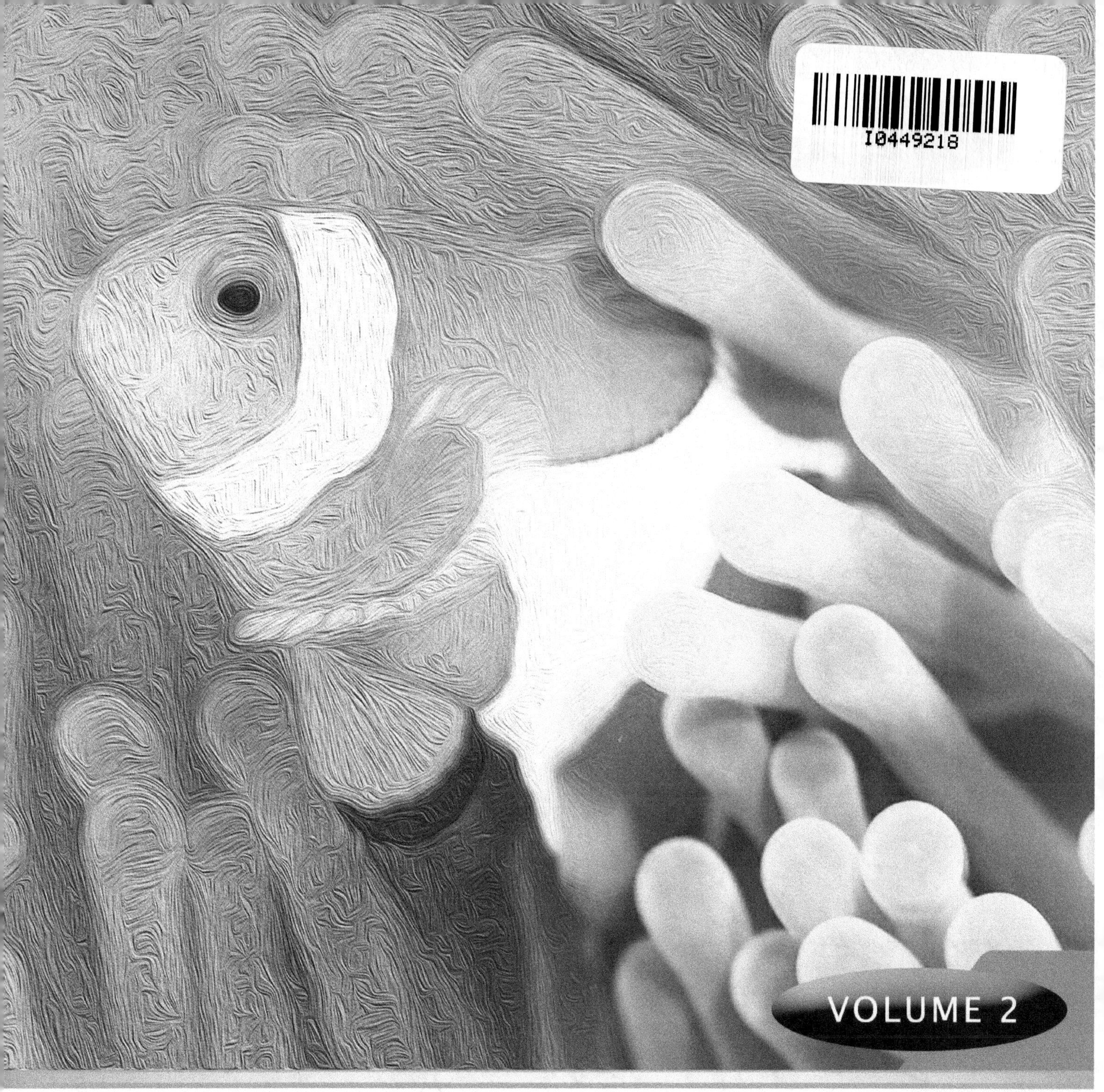

Sea Creatures
SHADING

A Grayscale Coloring Book

COLORING BOOK FOR ADULTS

COLOR TEST PAGE

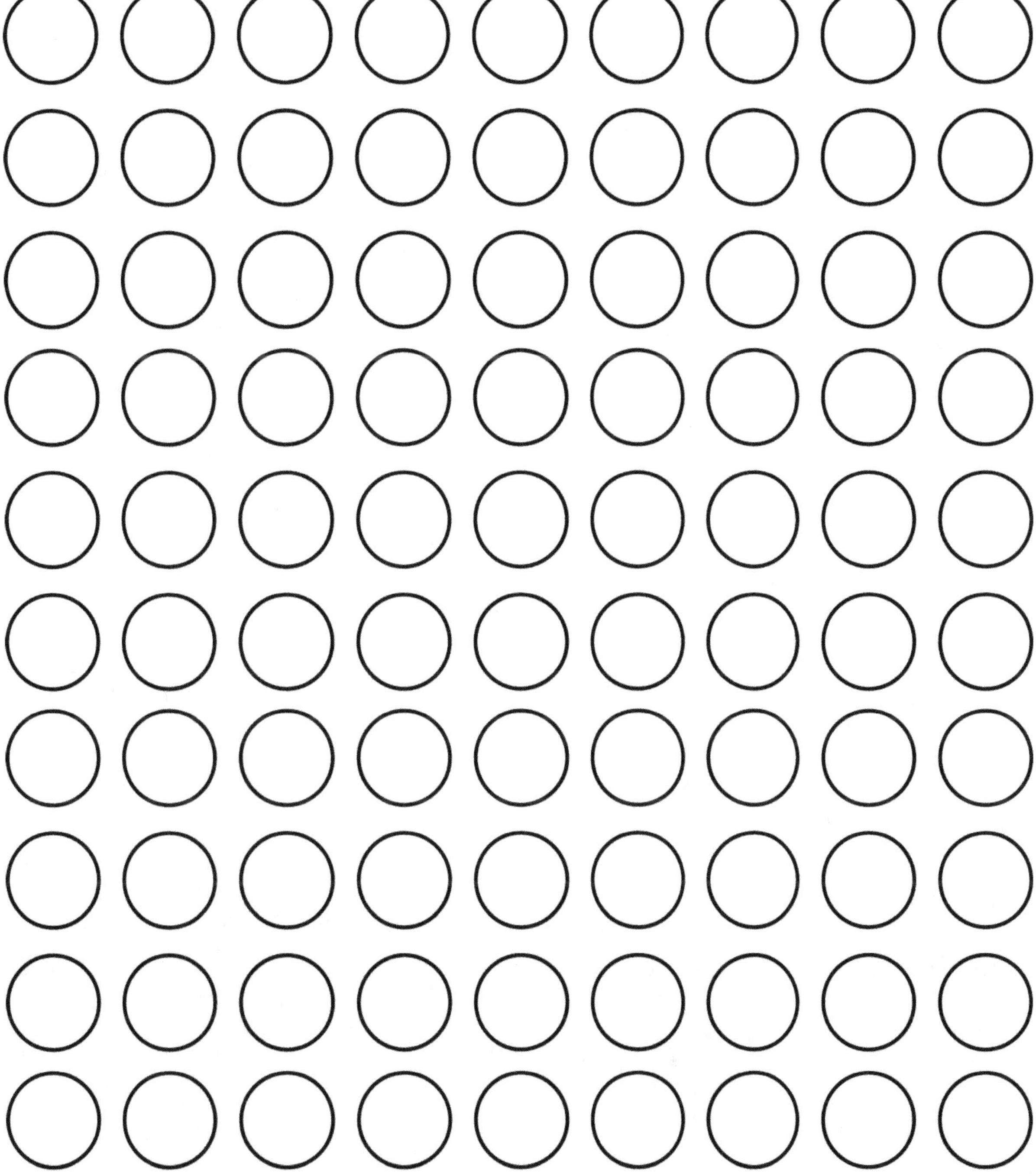

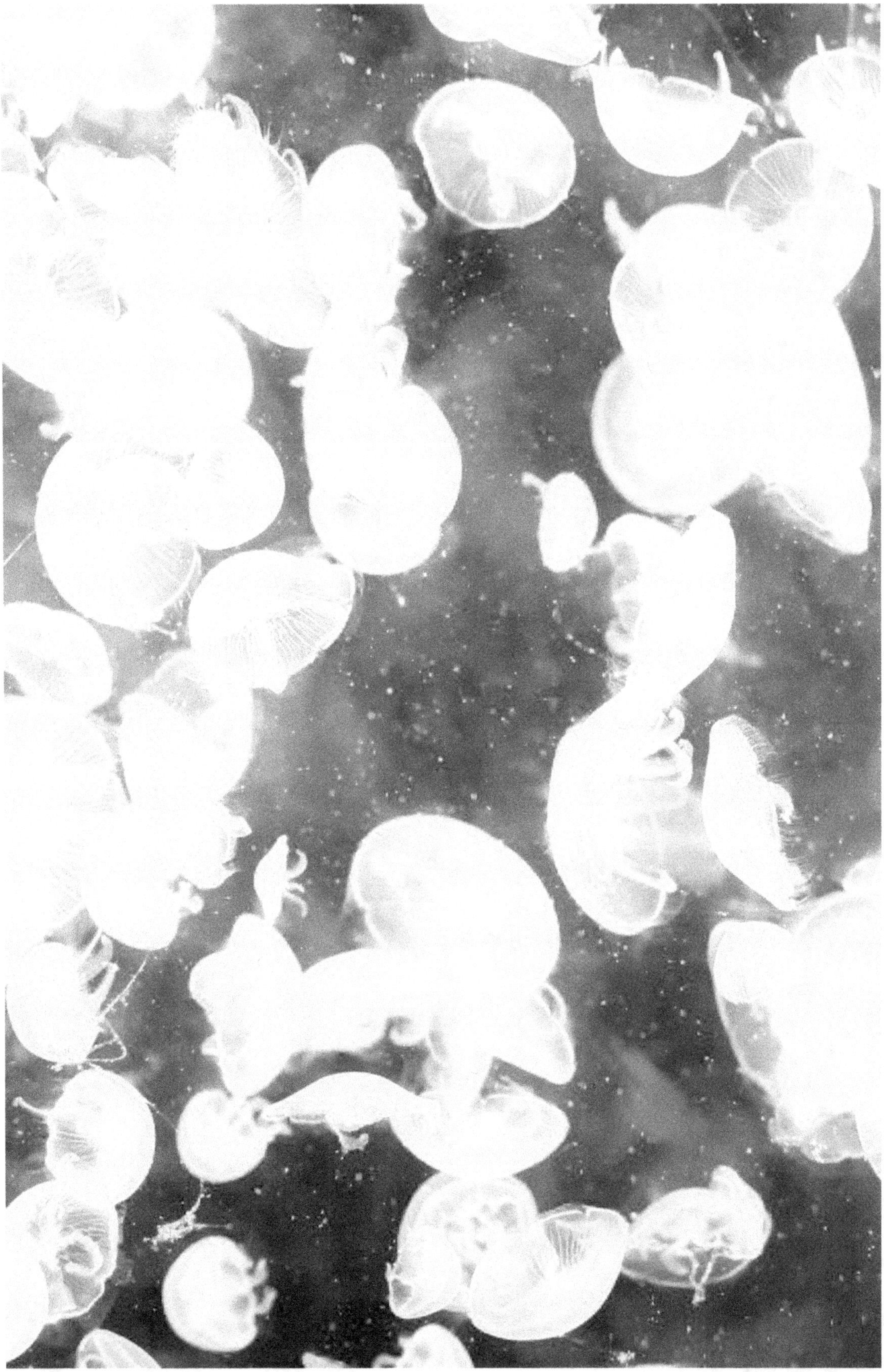

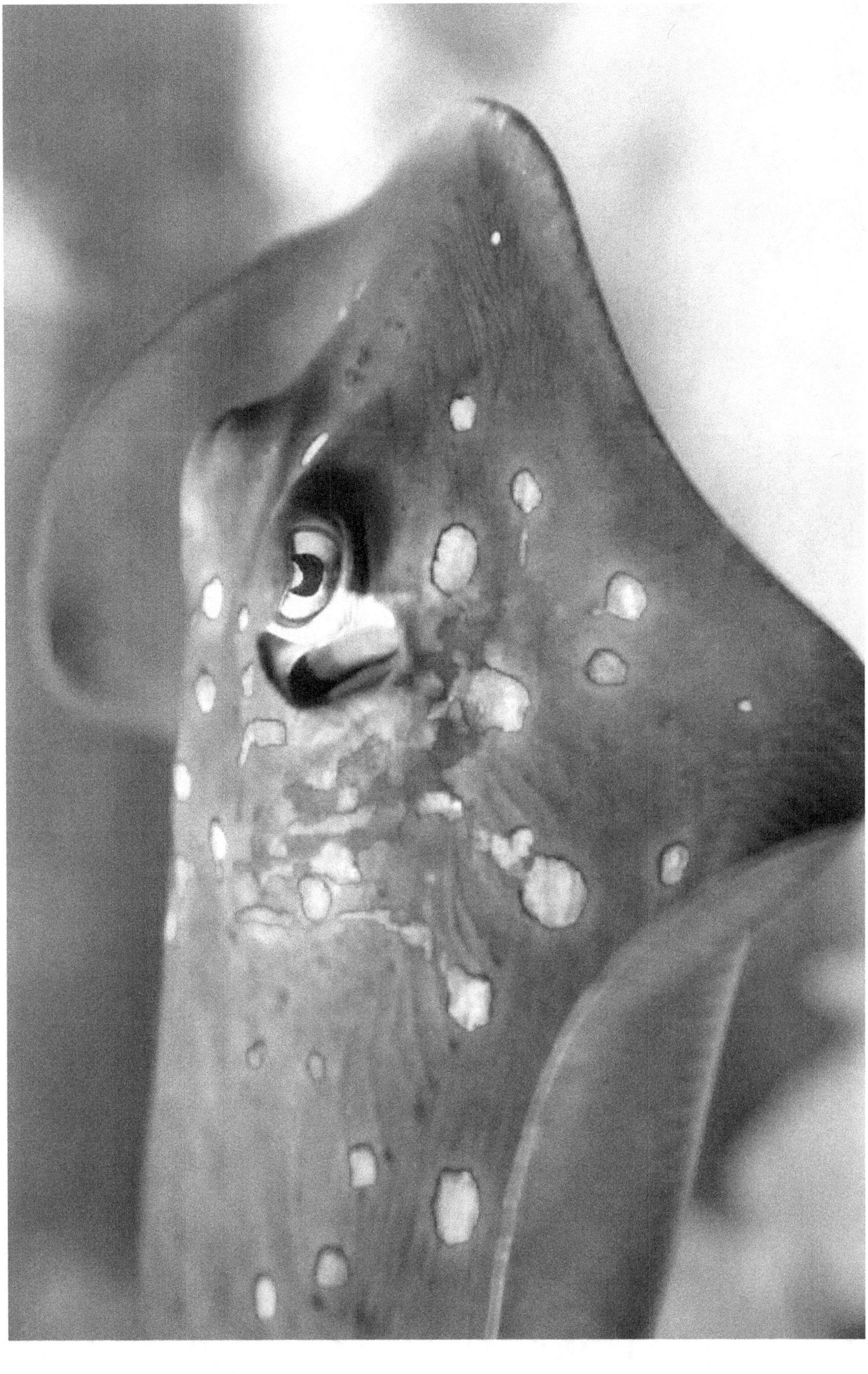

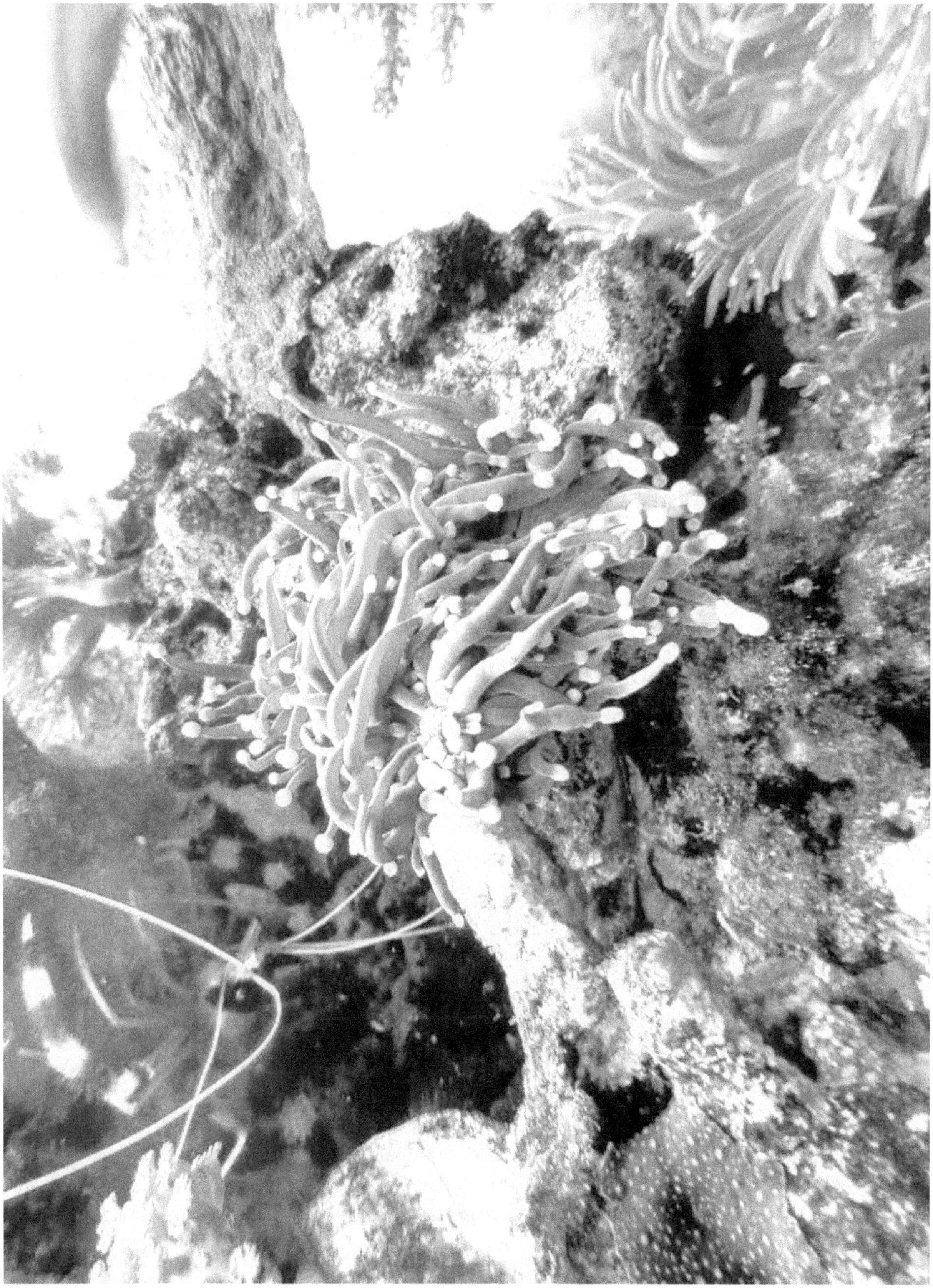

www.ingramcontent.com/pod-product-compliance
Lightning Source LLC
Chambersburg PA
CBHW052017280526
45793CB00005B/1016
9781535429283